The Nature and Science of
SUNLIGHT

Jane Burton and Kim Taylor

Gareth Stevens Publishing
MILWAUKEE

For a free color catalog describing Gareth Stevens Publishing's list of high-quality books and multimedia programs, call 1-800-542-2595 (USA) or 1-800-461-9120 (Canada). Gareth Stevens Publishing's Fax: (414) 225-0377. See our catalog, too, on the World Wide Web: http://gsinc.com

Library of Congress Cataloging-in-Publication Data

Burton, Jane.
The nature and science of sunlight / by Jane Burton and Kim Taylor.
p. cm. -- (Exploring the science of nature)
Includes index.
Summary: Examines the energy and light produced by the sun and their importance to life on Earth.
ISBN 0-8368-1946-2 (lib. bdg.)
1. Sun--Juvenile literature. 2. Solar radiation--Juvenile literature. 3. Light--Juvenile literature.
[1. Solar radiation. 2. Light.] I. Taylor, Kim. II. Title. III. Series: Burton, Jane.
Exploring the science of nature.
QB521.5.B87 1997   97-8481
523.7'2--dc21

First published in North America in 1997 by
Gareth Stevens Publishing
1555 North RiverCenter Drive, Suite 201
Milwaukee, Wisconsin 53212 USA

This U.S. edition © 1997 by Gareth Stevens, Inc. Created with original © 1997 by White Cottage Children's Books. Text and photographs © 1997 by Jane Burton and Kim Taylor. The photograph on page 12 (*top*) is courtesy of Robert Burton. Conceived, designed, and produced by White Cottage Children's Books, 29 Lancaster Park, Richmond, Surrey TW10 6AB, England. Additional end matter © 1997 by Gareth Stevens, Inc.

The right of Jane Burton and Kim Taylor to be identified as the authors of this work have been asserted by them in accordance with the Copyright, Design and Patents Act 1988. Educational consultant, Jane Weaver; scientific adviser, Dr. Jan Taylor.

Printed in the United States of America

1 2 3 4 5 6 7 8 9 01 00 99 98 97

Contents

Words that appear in the glossary are printed in **boldface** type the first time they occur in the text.

Radiant Sun

The Sun *(opposite)* is a gigantic ball of white-hot gases. It is more than one hundred times as wide as Earth. The Sun generates huge amounts of heat and light — like an enormous power station. The Sun's rays spread out in every direction. They are made of heat, light, radio waves, and other sorts of **radiation** that cannot be felt or seen. Energy from the Sun is in the form of **electromagnetic** waves. These waves spread out from the Sun like the ripples that form when a stone is dropped into a pond.

Electromagnetic waves travel in straight lines at 186,420 miles (300,000 kilometers) per second — the speed of light. It takes just eight minutes for the Sun's energy to reach Earth — a distance of 92 million miles (148 million km).

Electromagnetic waves can be far apart or close together. Radio waves can be more than a mile (km) apart, while waves of heat are separated by less than .0394 inch (1 millimeter). The distance between waves is called a **wavelength**. The wavelength of light is so small that it is measured in millionths of a millimeter.

Above: On a still winter's day, a mallard duck treads water and flaps its wings. This forms ripples in the water like the electromagnetic waves that spread out from the Sun.

Day and Night

The Earth is always spinning. It spins around once every twenty-four hours. When the side of Earth that you are on faces the Sun, it is daytime. Then, as Earth turns, the Sun seems to sink slowly until it disappears below the **horizon**. Then it is night where you are. The Sun shines on only half of Earth's surface. In that half, it is day. The other half is in **shadow**; it is night.

Imagine that Earth is like an orange. The peel of the orange is Earth's **atmosphere**. Rays from the Sun come straight down through Earth's atmosphere at midday, like a knife cutting straight through the orange peel. But in the early morning and again in the evening, the Sun's rays enter Earth's atmosphere at an angle. At an angle, the rays have to travel farther through the atmosphere before reaching Earth. That is why early morning

Right: Imagine Earth as an orange. The peel is Earth's atmosphere. The Sun's rays at midday go straight through Earth's atmosphere.

and evening sunshine is cooler than the sunshine that occurs at midday. The atmosphere has **filtered** out most of the heat.

Right: In the early morning and evening, the Sun's rays strike Earth at an angle. The rays must pass through more of the atmosphere at these times than at midday.

Above: As Earth turns on its **axis**, the Sun rises slowly in the sky. Here, the Sun has been photographed every six minutes to reveal this movement. The angle at which the Sun rises depends on the season of the year and the location of the observer. Wherever you are in the world, the Sun sets at the same angle to the horizon as it rose in the morning.

The Seasons

The spinning Earth travels through space at 33,556 miles (54,000 km) per hour in a giant circle around the Sun. This journey takes a year. Whether it is spring, summer, autumn, or winter depends on where Earth is on this long journey.

It is winter in the Northern **Hemisphere** when the **North Pole** is facing away from the Sun. Little light and warmth can get through Earth's atmosphere because the Sun's rays are striking that part of Earth at a narrow angle. Days are short, and nights are long. In the Northern Hemisphere, December 21 is known as the winter **solstice**. On that day, the Sun is at its lowest in the sky, and day length is at its shortest. After the winter solstice, days gradually get longer, and the Sun's rays feel stronger. June 21 is the summer solstice in the Northern Hemisphere. After that date, the days start to shorten again.

Above: In the warm spring sunshine, oak buds burst open, and bright new leaves unfold.

Above: In summer, oak trees are a dense mass of green leaves that soak up sunlight.

Right: In autumn, oak leaves and acorns fall to the ground.

Above: In winter, oak leaves on the damp ground sometimes become coated in white crystals of frost.

Opposite: The winter Sun sets, ending one of the shortest days of the year.

When it is winter in the Northern Hemisphere, it is summer in the Southern Hemisphere. When the south has its short days of winter, the north has long summer days. But twice each year, in spring and autumn, halfway between midsummer and midwinter, day and night are of equal length over almost the entire world. At the spring **equinox** and again at the autumn equinox, day and night are each twelve hours long.

At the **Equator**, day and night are nearly equal in length all through the year. The midday Sun shines from almost directly overhead. Its rays come straight through the atmosphere, and the weather is always hot. In many hot countries, there is no winter and no summer. Instead, there are rainy and dry seasons.

Right: It is late summer and near the start of the rainy season in the Kimberley region of Western Australia. These brilliantly colored flowers cast their shadows onto the baked red soil as the Sun climbs almost directly overhead.

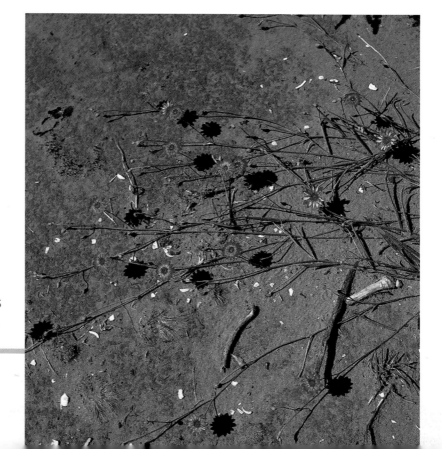

Right: Flowers called lesser celandine flourish in damp woods and hedges in the Arctic. On sunny days in early spring before the tree buds burst, the celandines open their bright flowers wide. They must set seed quickly before the trees overhead block the Sun.

Flowers of the Midnight Sun

The flower called the Arctic poppy grows near the North Pole. There, in midsummer, the days are so long that the Sun never sets at all. It is light all day and all night. The weather is often cloudy and cool, however. Summers are short, and the air never gets very warm.

Whenever the Sun does shine, the flowers of the Arctic poppy turn to face the Sun as it moves around the sky. The petals collect the sunshine to warm the middle of the flower. This extra warmth helps the poppies quickly produce seeds before the end of the short Arctic summer.

Opposite: The stems of Arctic poppies form a spiral because they grow faster on one side when the Sun shines. The spiral stems also allow the flowers to keep facing the Sun.

Sunshine Makes Sugar

Top: Grass provides food for millions of insects, such as this stripe-winged grasshopper. Grass is also the main food for many larger animals, from rabbits and hares to cattle and horses.

Below: An animal called the quokka munches on leaves of a wild fig tree at its home on the Western Australian island of Rottnest. Like kangaroos and many other Australian animals, quokkas are strictly vegetarian.

Huge quantities of energy come to Earth from the Sun. On average, nearly every 11 square feet (1 square meter) of Earth's surface receive about 1,000 **watts** of sunlight. This is the same as the light from ten strong light bulbs.

Life on Earth would not be possible without energy from the Sun. The Sun's heat warms the surface of Earth so that animals and plants can live. Plants use energy from sunlight to grow. Their green leaves collect a small part of the Sun's radiation and use it in a chemical process called **photosynthesis**. In this process, a gas called **carbon dioxide** from the air is combined with water in the leaves to make sugar. Sugar is the basic food for plants, and plants are the basic food for animals.

Opposite: A cockchafer beetle clings to the leaf of an oak tree. One oak tree provides food for millions of insects of many kinds, including caterpillars, plant bugs, beetles, bush crickets, and gall wasps.

Storing Energy

Energy from the Sun cannot easily be collected and stored for any length of time. This is because radiation from the Sun must be changed into **chemical energy** in order to produce food. Plants are able to change sunlight into chemical energy, but animals cannot. Plants use sunlight to make sugar as well as other energy-storing chemicals, such as **starch**. When you eat food, the stored energy from the food is released into your body so that you can work and play until you are hungry once again.

Many plants produce fruit. Some of the fruit becomes sweet and changes color as it ripens in the Sun. Some berries and apples turn red so that animals can see the fruit is ready for eating. Not only do the animals eat the fruit, they also do the important job of spreading the seeds.

Top: A gray squirrel has found treasure in a sweet, ripened apple.

Opposite: Apples ripen best in the Sun. The sunniest side of each of this particular kind of apple turns the reddest. Apples hidden among leaves often stay green.

Above: The apple this squirrel has been gnawing on is so ripe it falls. The squirrel will have to finish its meal on the ground.

17

Keeping Warm

Mammals and birds are warm-blooded. This means they are able to keep their bodies warm, even when the air is cold. Their muscles make heat all the time, using chemical energy stored in the food they eat. Cold-blooded animals cannot do this. They need to **bask** in the sunshine to keep warm.

A basking animal spreads its body out so that it catches the maximum amount of sunshine. It

Below: A purple hairstreak butterfly basks with its wings spread to catch the most warmth from the Sun.

holds itself as flat as possible at **right angles** to the Sun's rays. Only when the muscles of a cold-blooded animal are warm enough will they work properly. Many cold-blooded animals have to warm up before they can fly or run.

Certain snakes and lizards change color when they are basking. Their skin becomes dark because dark-colored surfaces absorb heat better than light-colored surfaces. Many warm-blooded animals also bask in the Sun. Using the Sun's heat to keep warm saves their energy.

Above: A cormorant that has swallowed some cold fish needs to warm up before the meal will digest. The bird spreads its wings to catch as much heat from the Sun as possible. It may also flap its wings at the same time so that its wing muscles create even more heat.

Rainbow Colors

Yellow is a "sunny" color, and sunlight is thought of as golden in color. But light from the Sun is colorless. It is known as white light. White light is a mix of all the colors of the rainbow — red, orange, yellow, green, blue, indigo, and violet. Each color has a particular wavelength. Red has the longest wavelength and violet the shortest.

The various colors of sunlight can be seen with a **prism**. A prism **refracts**, or bends, light. It bends each color at a slightly different angle, so the colors separate. Drops of water sometimes act as natural prisms, refracting sunlight into its separate colors. When you see a water drop glinting brilliantly in the Sun, move your head slightly from side to side until you see the drop change color (*see page 29*).

Opposite: A rainbow arches over a huge flock of lesser flamingos wading in a lake at evening. Rainbows only appear in the sky when the Sun is low. If the Sun is more than 41 degrees above the horizon, the rainbow disappears into the ground.

Sunlight does not shine straight through a glass prism. It is bent at an angle.

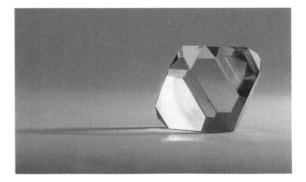

When light strikes one face of a prism at a sharp angle, it is separated into the colors of the rainbow.

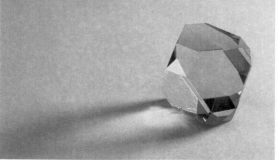

The particular color that is visible depends on the angle between the Sun, the prism, and the observer's eye.

Move your head just a fraction to change the angle, and the color will also change.

Invisible Rays

Top: A kingcup looks yellow to humans. But insects see a starlike ultraviolet pattern in the middle of the flower.

Opposite: Warmth from the Sun melts the snow. Water drops on branches of silver birch trees glisten in the light of the Sun. A special "starburst" filter on the camera produces rainbow-colored sunbeams.

Above and right: Cats and rabbits enjoy basking in the Sun. The oil on their ears produces Vitamin D in the sunlight. The animals ingest the vitamin during grooming.

Living things cannot survive without the light and warmth of the Sun. But the Sun also produces rays that can be harmful. **Ultraviolet** rays from the Sun bombard Earth's atmosphere. Most of them are soaked up by a layer of what is known as **ozone**, high above the clouds. But some of the ultraviolet radiation gets through the ozone. Ultraviolet radiation causes sunburn and skin cancer.

Humans cannot see ultraviolet light, but insects and birds can. Some plants even produce flowers that reflect an ultraviolet pattern to attract insects, such as bees.

The Sun's ultraviolet light benefits living things, as well. The human body uses ultraviolet radiation to make **Vitamin D**, which is necessary for bones to grow. When furry animals sunbathe, Vitamin D is made in the oil on their fur. They lick the vitamin off during grooming.

Sky Blue

Most of the light from the Sun comes straight through the atmosphere to Earth's surface (*opposite*). But a small fraction of the Sun's light is **scattered** by the **molecules** of oxygen in the air. These molecules are invisible, but some of the scattered light bouncing off them can be seen. Although only a little of the Sun's light is scattered by the air, it is enough to make the sky look blue.

Astronauts visiting the Moon see the Sun shining out of a black sky. This sunshine is dangerous because the Moon has no atmosphere to scatter light or to stop ultraviolet rays.

Right: Butterflies and dragonflies do not fly at all when the weather is cool. They need the Sun to shine before they can fly or eat.

The Setting Sun

Top: As the Sun goes down, **diurnal** creatures, such as this Australian gumleaf grasshopper, rest.

The atmosphere at Earth's horizon contains smoke and dust. As the Sun sets, its rays of light have to pass through the smoke and dust. Yellow, orange, and red light get through smoke and dust much easier than the other colors. So the Sun often looks reddish when it is low on the horizon. When the rays are further reflected by clouds, a beautiful, fiery splendor appears.

Below: After dark, **nocturnal** creatures like this toad emerge from their cool, dark hiding places.

Opposite: The Sun sets on the horizon. Smoke and dust in the air near Earth's surface filter out blue and green light from the Sun. Only the warm colors of yellow, orange, and red remain.

26

Activities:

Energy and Color

Sunshine is made of light, heat, and other radiation that travel through space at high speed. When the radiation reaches Earth's atmosphere, most of it travels straight through the air to reach the ground. When the Sun shines, you can see its brilliant light and feel its heat. Light and heat are forms of energy used by plants and animals. Without energy from the Sun, there would be almost no life on Earth.

Above and below: Objects that are pale in color reflect heat and light from the Sun.

Soaking up Energy

Heat and light are reflected by pale-colored surfaces and absorbed by dark-colored ones. That is why white sand on a beach is cool to the touch, even in strong sunshine — while black sand is impossible to walk upon.

Above: Dark-colored objects, such as these pebbles, absorb heat and light from the Sun.

Most beaches have pebbles of many different colors. Select some of the darkest and some of the palest that you can find. Leave your pebbles in the Sun for a while and then touch them. Which feels the warmest, and which the coolest?

To show how black surfaces absorb heat and pale surfaces reflect heat, find two empty cans, some black and white paints, and a thermometer that can be placed in water. Paint the outside of one can black and the other white. Fill each to the same level with water and leave them side by side in the Sun for a couple of hours. Then measure the temperature of the water in the cans, making sure you leave the thermometer in each can until the reading is steady. Which of the cans works best as a **solar** heater?

Splitting Sunlight into Colors

Just as heat and light are forms of radiation with different wavelengths, so each color of light has its own particular wavelength. When all the colors are mixed together, light appears colorless and is known as "white light." The colors of sunshine can be separated with a prism. This is because each color is bent by the prism at a slightly different angle. A shaft of white light entering the prism on one side comes out as a fan of brilliant rainbow colors on the other side.

A prism does not always have to be made of glass. Water will work well as a prism, too. You can make your own water prism using a mirror. First, find a small rectangular mirror, one that is preferably not installed in a frame. Fill a rectangular dish with water. Put the dish on the floor in the middle of a room that has a sunny window. Place the mirror in it so that it rests against one side of the dish (*see the illustration below*). The best angle for the mirror depends on how high the Sun is in the sky. Experiment with various angles to create the most effective prism.

The water prism works best when the Sun is fairly low in the sky, so try this experiment in the morning or evening. Draw the curtains so a thin shaft of sunlight falls onto the mirror. Adjust the angle of the mirror, and turn the dish slowly until a rainbow appears on the wall beside or beneath the window (*see below*). The rainbow will look best on a pure white surface, so try "catching" it on a sheet of white paper.

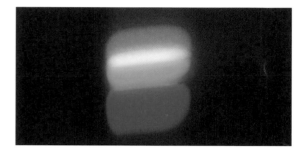

Raindrops also act like prisms. A rainbow is formed by thousands of the little water prisms falling through the air, each giving flashes of color as they pass through the special "rainbow" angle of 41 degrees between your eye, the rainbow, and the Sun. Even though the drops fall quickly, the rainbow stays still. You can see this effect on a sunny day by turning on a garden hose that has a fine spray. The rainbow formed does not move with the drops of the spray but stays still — until you move, and then it moves with you.

Below: A rainbow forms in the spray of a garden hose.

Above: The mirror acts as one face of a prism, and the water surface acts as another.

Glossary

atmosphere: the layer of gases that surrounds a planet.

axis: the imaginary line through the middle of an object around which it turns.

bask: to rest in the Sun.

carbon dioxide: a gas that is a combination of carbon and oxygen.

chemical energy: the energy associated with the formation and breaking down of chemical bonds.

diurnal: active in the daytime.

electromagnetic: the form in which waves of heat, light, and other sorts of energy travel through space.

Equator: the imaginary line around the center of Earth.

equinox: the time of year when the Sun is directly over the Equator, and day and night are of equal length.

filter: to stop some parts but allow other parts to pass through.

hemisphere: one half of a globe, such as planet Earth.

horizon: the line where land and sea appear to meet the sky.

mammals: warm-blooded, furry animals that produce milk for their young.

molecules: the smallest parts of a substance, made up of two or more atoms that are joined.

nocturnal: active in the nighttime.

North Pole: the point in the Northern Hemisphere around which Earth rotates.

ozone: a form of oxygen in which the molecules are made up of three, instead of the normal two, oxygen atoms. There is a layer of ozone in Earth's upper atmosphere. It helps protect our planet from the Sun's harmful ultraviolet rays.

photosynthesis: a process in which plants use energy from the Sun to make food.

prism: glass, a raindrop, or another transparent material that refracts light into the colors of the rainbow.

radiation: energy that travels in straight lines from a source.

refract: to bend.

right angle: the angle at the corner of a square or a rectangle.

scattered: bounced in all directions.

shadow: an area not lit by the Sun.

solar: relating to the Sun.

solstice: the time when the Sun is at its greatest distance from the Equator.

starch: a food material, closely related to sugar, that is stored in plants.

ultraviolet rays: radiation with wavelengths shorter than visible light.

Vitamin D: a complex chemical, essential to the growth of bones.

watts: units of power in the metric system. A strong electric light bulb uses 100 watts.

wavelength: the distance between waves. The lengths of the distances vary depending on the type of wave.

Plants and Animals

The common names of plants and animals vary from language to language. But plants and animals also have scientific names, based on Greek or Latin words, that are the same the world over. Each plant and animal has two scientific names. The first name is called the genus. It starts with a capital letter. The second name is the species name. It starts with a small letter.

Arctic poppy (*Papaver radicatum*) — northern Europe, Arctic 12-13

cockchafer (*Melolantha melolantha*) — Europe 14-15

common toad (*Bufo bufo*) — Europe, similar species worldwide 26

European rabbit (*Oryctolagus cuniculus*) — Europe, northern Africa, and introduced to Australia and New Zealand 22

four-spotted chaser dragonfly (*Libelula quadrimaculata*) — Europe 24

gray squirrel (*Sciurus carolinensis*) — North America, Great Britain 17

gumleaf grasshopper (*Goniaea australiae*) — Australia 26

Iceland poppy (*Papaver nudicanle*) — Asia, introduced elsewhere 32

illyarie (*Eucalyptus erythrocorys*) — Western Australia 30

impala (*Aepyceros melampus*) — southern Africa 10-11

kingcup (marsh marigold) (*Caltha palustris*) — Europe 22

lesser celandine (*Ranunculus ficaria*) — Europe 12-13

lesser flamingo (*Phoenicopterue minor*) — southern and eastern Africa, northwestern India 10-11, 20-21

mallard (*Anas platyrhynchos*) — Europe, North America 5

pedunculate oak (*Quercus robur*) — Europe, southwestern Asia, North Africa 8-9

purple hairstreak butterfly (*Quercusia quercus*) — Europe 18

quokka (*Setonix brachyurus*) — Australia 14

silver birch (*Betula pendula*) — Europe, Asia Minor, introduced elsewhere 22-23

stripe-winged grasshopper (*Stenobothrus lineatus*) — Europe 14

white-necked cormorant (*Phalacrocorax carbo*) — Africa 19

Books to Read

How to Build a Sun. Spencer R. Weart (Coward McCann)

Light. Science Works! series. S. Parker (Gareth Stevens)

Our Amazing Sun. Richard C. Adams (Troll Associates)

Our Friend, the Sun. Janet Palazzo-Craig (Troll Associates)

Our Star — The Sun. Robert Estalella (Barron's Educational Series)

The Sun and Its Secrets. Isaac Asimov (Gareth Stevens)

The Sun Is Always Shining Somewhere. Allan Fowler (Childrens Press)

The Sun and Moon. Patrick Moore (Copper Beech)

Videos and Web Sites

Videos

The Amazing Vanishing Ozone.
    (PBS Video)
Energy From the Sun. (Encyclopædia
    Britannica Educational Corporation)
Learning About Solar Energy.
    (AIMS Media)
Photosynthesis. (Phoenix/BFA)
A Piece of Sunshine. (Phoenix/BFA)

Web Sites

www.windows.umich.edu/photoscience.la.
    asu.edu/photosyn/study.html
www.earthsky.com/./1996/es960313.html
www.deltatech.com/deltatech/rainbowx.
    html
www.mala.bc.ca/~mcneil/sci.htx
www.energy.ca.gov/education/
www.discovery.com

Index